BEAD JEWELRY FOR

BEGINNERS

An Essential Guide to Learning How
to Make Bead Jewelry

Copyright@2023

Jane Lukeman

Table of Contents

CHAPTER ONE

EVERYTHING YOU NEED TO UNDERSTAND ABOUT BEADS

Beads are little items of ornamentation that are most frequently employed in the creation of jewelry. Beads typically need to have a hole bored in them before they can be used and this allows thread to be threaded through the beads, which in turn allows the beads to be strung together on a string or wire. Nevertheless, beads can also be glued to the surfaces of a variety of products such as wall hangings and sculptures; in this case, the surfaces do not need to be punctured in order for the beads

4

to be used. Beads are versatile enough to be employed in a variety of applications, including accessorizing personal objects like handbags and purses. In addition to that, you can find them in things around the house like cushions and tablecloths.

Beads come in a wide range of sizes, from extremely tiny beads that are difficult to manipulate without the use of specialized equipment to extremely huge beads with a diameter of more than one centimeter.

Glass, plastic, and stone are the three types of materials that are most frequently used to create beads. Nevertheless, beads can also be crafted from a wide variety of other materials, such as bone, coral, pearl, wood, porcelain, fiber, paper, seeds, gemstones, metal clay, polymer clay, and synthetic materials. As you can see, you have a wide variety of options available to you when it comes to selecting the materials with which you would like to work.

Beadwork is the term used to describe the process of creating something using beads. Beadwork can be accomplished in a variety of ways, the most common of which include stringing, jewelry, embroidery, crochet, knitting, loom weaving, and off-loom weaving.

Beadwork is a craft that can be practiced by hobbyists of varying skill levels. Beaders new to the craft can create even the most basic examples of beaded jewelry in almost little time at all. Examples include necklaces, bracelets, and earrings.

Note

It is imperative that you do not become perplexed by the term "seed bead." It does not necessary signify that the bead is manufactured from seeds, however it is true that some beads are made from seeds. The word "seed bead" is a catch-all phrase that is frequently used to refer to any little bead.

Brief History About Bead

Since the beginning of known civilization, people have been using beads and they have been around for a very long time. The earliest known examples of jewelry are a pair of beads formed from the shells of sea snails. These beads are estimated to be roughly 100,000 years old. Beads have a variety of uses, including those in the realm of jewelry and personal decoration, as well as those in religious practice.

Beads have been used in every culture that has been studied as a form of art, prayer, and as a marker of an individual's social standing. The exact date of the beginning of the history of beads is unknown; nevertheless, one thing is certain: beads have been used, and some of the world's first artwork was likely created with beads.

The area of the world in which the beads were first produced had a significant amount of impact on the kinds of materials that were utilized to make the beads. In the beginning, people used anything from plant seeds to bones to different kinds of stones. Prayer beads are still used in modern times and can be purchased in a variety of materials, including plastic, wood, and glass, to cater to the needs of those who practice a wide variety of faiths.

Beadwork is still an essential component of civilization in this day and age. The art and passion of beadwork will continue to be an essential component of each and every culture on the face of the planet, in a variety of forms, including the mass production of a wide variety of beads for use in religious goods, jewelry, and craft projects, as well as the handcrafted creation of creative glass beads and lampwork.

CHAPTER TWO

BASIC BEGINNER BEADING TOOLS

Beading is a fun and creative way to expand your design repertoire and making your own beaded jewelry is a great way to get started. When it comes to beading, there are an almost infinite number of things that can be created, and there lot of tools available to help you make anything your imagination can conjure up!

The fundamental equipment you'll require to get started with beadwork are listed below!

1. Set of Pliers

When making any kind of jewelry, having pliers available in your toolkit is an extremely helpful tool. There is a handy set of useful pliers available that has all of the necessary pliers for the production of jewelry as well as the stringing of beads. You can also buy each pair of pliers independently, but the most important thing is that you are familiar with how to use all of the different sets of pliers correctly.

Chain Nose

While opening and closing jump rings, the chain nose is the tool of choice.

Round Nose

The round nose is utilized in the process of wrapping wires and making connections.

2. Wire Cutters

These are the cutters that you can use to cut wires and threads in a precise manner so that your work remains tidy.

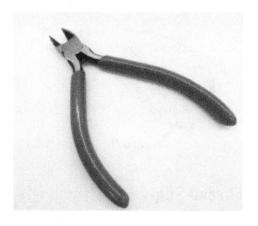

3. Scissors

Beaders of jewelry are required to have a pair of little, pointed, and extremely sharp scissors in their toolset. Not only are they used for cutting thread, but they are also useful for maneuvering into tight trim areas when working on bead embroidery.

4. Thread Snips

Beaded thread, delicate wires, textiles, yarn, and a wide variety of other materials can all be easily cut with thread snips.

Thread snips have a spring-loaded mechanism that makes them easier to use, even in places that are difficult to access. After cutting, you'll have a neat finish thanks to the strong blades' ability to hold a sharp edge. In the same way that you would use scissors, thread snips are put to use in the same way.

5. Beads Mat

This practical bead mat is constructed from a unique fleecy fabric that features fibers that stop beads from rolling away from the surface of the mat.

The bead mat prevents little objects from rolling away and disappearing, which is a common occurrence because of their tendency to do so. You will save yourself a lot of time and irritation by not having to crawl about looking for that stray bead if you drop a little bead on it since it will just remain put.

6. Beads Needles for Stringing beads

Bead stringing can be made easier with these miniature, flexible, twisted wire needles. A retractable eye on each needle makes it ideal for threading tiny beads.

They make it a lot simpler to string a number of beads onto a thin thread, even if the holes in the beads are quite tiny.

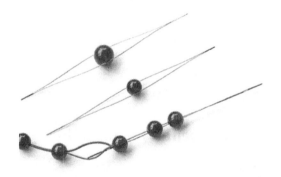

7. Bead Board

The bead board fulfills a requirement for beaders and was developed with the mobile beader in mind. Make use of it to plan out your jewelry designs and make any required adjustments before you begin stringing the components.

The bead board will come in beneficial on a variety of scenarios, from matching colors to ensuring precision with the measuring guides, to constructing various thread designs and staying organized.

CHAPTER THREE

CREATING CERAMIC BEADS PATTERN BRACELET

If you do enjoy Ceramic beads, here is a bracelet made entirely out of Ceramic for you to wear. This bracelet, which features black seed beads and ceramic beads, is both sophisticated and traditional. The instructions that are provided below will walk you through the process of making this bracelet.

Step 1

Supplies You'll Need

1. Round Porcelain Ceramic Bead Strands Measuring 8mm

2. Glass Seed Beads of size 12/0, in black

3. Round Acrylic Beads 3mm Light Golden Plated

4. String material with a thickness of 0.2mm Nylon Fishing Thread (white)

5. Iron Jump Rings ranging in size from 4 to 10mm

6. Elite clasps

Step 2

Assemble the First Section of the Seed Beads Bracelet

1. Snip off a length of white nylon wire, thread 10 black seed beads with a 2mm diameter onto the wire, and then cross the 2 wires over the seed beads and pull tight.

2. Cross a pin over the seed beads; thread 5 black seed beads of 2mm onto the wire; a 3mm light golden plated bead correspondingly along with the 8mm ceramic bead onto the wire in the center. Thread a 3mm light golden plated bead along with 5 black seed beads of 2mm onto the wire.

3. Cross the ends of the wire over the pin seed bead;

4. Continue to add four 2mm black seed beads, a 3mm light golden plated bead correspondingly along the 8mm ceramic bead onto the wire, and then repeat the methods from the previous steps.

Step 3

Finish up with the Bracelet

1. continue following this pattern until you reach the desired length; for this bracelet, I use 17 Porcelain Ceramic beads.

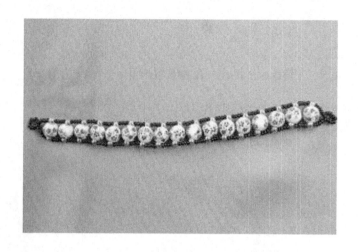

2. Next, thread a jump ring and the other part of the clasp onto the wire and then connect the bracelet.

Step 4

Take a look at the finished product of this porcelain ceramic bracelet:

CHAPTER FOUR

CONSTRUCTING A LOVELY BRACELET WITH GLASS ROUND BEADS

In the following guide, I will demonstrate how you can fashion a brand new and enticing bracelet out of glass beads. When I was making this bracelet with glass beads, I used the woven pattern that is traditionally used for friendship bracelets. Bracelets made of beads, particularly glass beads, have a great deal of texture and are very attractive. People are always interested in bracelets with glass beads, and bracelets with glass beads are fashionable during any season. Follow the instructions below to create this bracelet using glass beads.

Supplies You'll Need

1. Crystal Glass Beads Measuring 8mm

2. Crystal Glass Beads Measuring 6mm

3. Seed Beads Measuring 4mm

4. Jump Rings measuring 14mm by 8mm

5. Jewelry String with a Width of 0.4mm

6. Supplies for Jewelry Tools and Equipment

7. Magnetic Closures for Jewelry

Step 1

Assemble The First Segment Of The Bracelet Using The Glass Beads.

1. Thread 12 seed beads onto the jewelry string, and then crossly add 1

crystal glass bead measuring 8mm,

and then tighten

2. Attach a crystal glass bead

measuring 6mm on each side

individually, and then pass the

jewelry string through 5 seed beads.

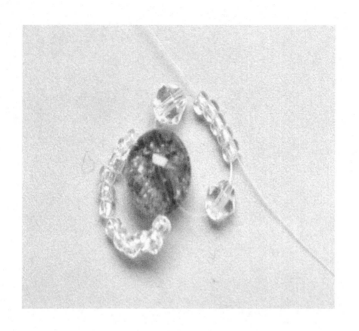

Step 2

Complete The Ship That Is Part Of The Bracelet.

1. Repeat the second step from the previous steps above to make a main beaded chain;

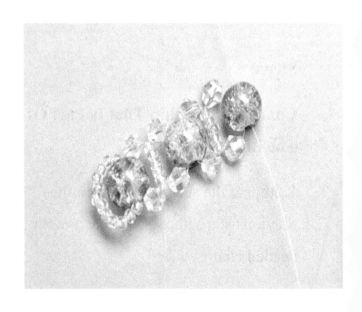

2. After entering the appropriate length of the beaded chain, then the jewelry string will cross into 12 4mm seed beads; attach the one litter jump ring to both ends of the beaded chain;

3. Attach two large jump rings, a link, and a claw clasp to one end of the chain, then attach a lobster claw clasp to the other end of the chain.

Step 3

The finished piece of jewelry should
look just like the image shown below.

CHAPTER FIVE

MAKING A BEADED WAVE PATTERN BRACELET

Beads made of crystal and pearls are always fashionable at any time of the year. Here I'll demonstrate how to make a beaded bracelet in the wave style using red glass beads and white pearl beads. The fact that the entire process requires part of your time gives the impression that it is challenging. Yet after you get started with the first few stages, you could realize that it's not that difficult.

Step 1

Supplies You'll Need

1. White pearl glass bead measuring 4mm

2. Glass crystal beads measuring 4mm

3. Antique silver Toggle clasps Tibetan style 14x11x2mm

4. Silver wire guardian wire protector 5 x 4.1 x 1.1mm

5. Transparent clear fishing threads nylon wire (0.2mm)

6. Thread Snips

Step 2

Instructions for Making the Bracelet 1:

1. Take a silver toggle clasp and thread it into the 0.2mm nylon fishing wire.

2. insert a bead made of red crystal glass and then cross the thread in the hole of the bead.

3. Attach a bead made of red crystal to the wire on your right, and attach a bead made of white pearl to the wire on your left. The next step is to take one additional red crystal bead and form a cross in the hole of the bead.

Note

A pearl bead will be located on the left, and there will be three red crystal beads around the pearl beads.

4. After that, you should carry out the third step once more. Nevertheless, you should put the white pearl beads to the wire on the right this time, and the red crystal bead should go on the wire on the left. After that, you need to construct a cross in the hole of the bead by threading one additional red crystal bead through it.

Step 3

Instruction for Making the Bracelet 2

1. To create the bracelet as long as you want it to be, you should repeat the above step (step 2) multiple times. Keep in mind that you need to thread the pearl beads and crystal beads across so that the beads can be arranged to seem like waves.

2. Add 3 additional white pearl beads, and arrange them so that they surround the red crystal bead on the left.

3. Move the thread to the bracelet's right side and add 3 more white pearl beads. Then you will notice the wave of the pearl beads moving across.

4. After completing the previous procedures, the wave bracelet is complete when the clasp is attached.

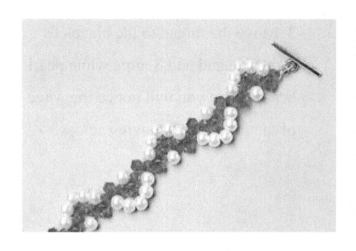

Step 4

Here is the completed Bracelet

CHAPTER SIX

MAKING ACRYLIC PEARL EARRINGS

Do you long to adorn your ears with a pair of pearl earrings that are both stunning and graceful? Here is a straightforward and understandable instruction on how to construct a pair of earrings.

Supplies You'll Need

1. Acrylic Beads Bark with an Orange Color, 21 x 5Millimeters in Diameter

2. Blue and white glass beads measuring 8 x 6 millimeters

3. Pink pearl beads measuring 8mm in diameter Beaded pearls made of white glass

4. Jewelry Iron Eyepins Measuring 450.7mm

5. Mix Iron Headpins

6. Earring Hooks in Silver Brass Measuring 19mm

7. Pliers

8. Wire cutters

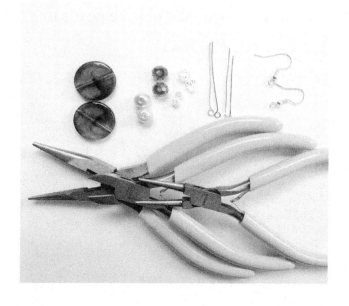

Step1

Create 2 beaded dangle patterns

1. Attach the pink pearl to a pin and create a loop on one of the sides of the pearl. Attach the pink pearl to the mixed iron headpins by sliding it onto

the pins, and then link the pearls to each other as shown.

2. Attach the transparent glass beads, the white pearl beads, the blue glass beads, and the orange glass beads to the jewelry finding iron eyepins in the correct order.

Now construct a loop at the other end
of the eyepin.

Step 2

Complete The Acrylic Pearl Earrings.

1. Attach a dangling hook to the top of the dangle, and then join the two beaded dangle patterns.

To make the other acrylic pearl earring, repeat the techniques outlined in the previous steps above.

Step 3

The finished Jewelry product should look just like the image below:

CHAPTER SEVEN

MAKING DROP BEADED PATTERN EARRINGS

Making beaded drop earrings with glass beads and gemstone beads is a simple and straightforward do-it-yourself craft. Earrings are the most common and popular piece of jewelry for women and girls, and they are suited for all seasons. Glass beads and gemstone beads both have a very rough surface and a very shiny surface. Be sure to pay attention to the instructions so that you can quickly and easily obtain your drop beaded earrings which feature gemstone beads and glass beads.

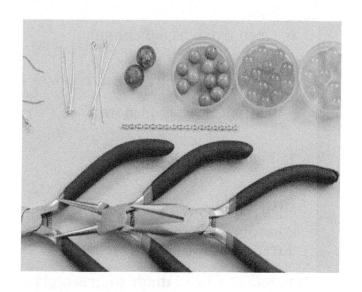

Supplies You'll Need

1. Cracked Glass Beads measuring 10mm

2. Jade Glass Beads measuring 8mm

3. Gemstone Beads measuring 8mm

4. Hooks for Earrings

5. Chain for Creating Jewelry

6. Open Eye pins 0.6x30mm

7. Jewelry head pins measuring 0.6 x 330mm made of golden iron

8. Pliers

Step 1

First, use headpins to string together a bead made of green glass and a gemstone bead.

1. Thread a 10mm glass bead onto an open eye pin, then form a loop at the end of the pin;

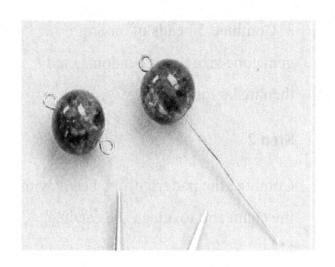

2. Combine 3 beads of a light green color and 3 beads of a thick green hue using headpins, then make loops;

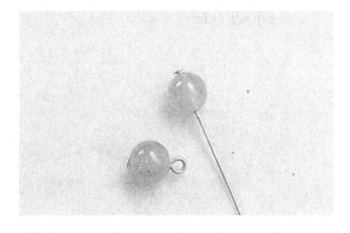

3. Combine 5 beads of an 8mm gemstone size using headpins, and then make loops.

Step 2

Combine the pattern of the beads with the chain and to attach the earring hooks.

1. Attach the appropriate golden chain to the 10mm glass bead pattern on one side, and attach the earring hook on the other side;

2. attach three 8mm light green color glass bead patterns to the golden chain, and attach 3 thick green color 8mm glass bead to the golden chain pattern, and then attach 5 8mm gemstone beads pattern to the golden chain pattern in order;

3. Repeat the steps above to make another pair of drop earrings.

Step 3

The final earring piece should look just like the image shown below.

CHAPTER EIGHT

MAKING PEARLS EARRINGS IN ANGLE PATTERN

Pearl beads are an excellent choice for use in the creation of earrings and virtually all women have at least one pair of earrings stored away in their jewelry boxes. To successfully complete these earrings made of pearl beads, simply follow these instructions.

Step 1

Supplies You'll Need

1. Glass Pearl Beads measuring 4mm

2. Golden Brass Hooks for earrings
Hooks for Ear Wires

3. Strands of Glass Pearl Beads
Measuring 6mm

4. Eye Pin made of Stainless Steel
Measuring 30mm

5. Strands of yellow lampwork beads
measuring 7-8 mm

6. Pliers

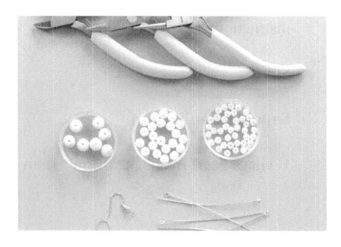

Step 2

**Create a Design for the Earrings
Using Beads**

1. String 4 glass pearl beads
measuring 6 mm using the eye pin,
and then cross the two ends of the pin;

2. thread a white pearl bead, a yellow
lampwork bead and a white pearl
bead onto the eye pin, and then cross
the two ends of the pin;

3. Construct two strands of pearl
beads as well as 8 strands of pearl
lampwork beads;

4. Join the two ends of one string of
pearl beads and 4 strings of lampwork
beads, as shown in the image below.

Step 3

Complete the pearls earrings.

1. string one glass pearl bead measuring 6mm in diameter onto the eye pin, and then cross the two ends of the pin;

2. secure the bead string in place at the corner that is opposite the corner where the beads string was made in step 2;

3. Following the instructions provided in the image, attach the earring hooks to the string of beads.

Step 4

The final earring piece should look just like the image shown below.

CHAPTER NINE

ROYAL BLUE BEADED COLOR SCHEME NECKLACE

The majority of the blue beads that make up this ocean-inspired necklace are cat eye beads in royal blue and seed beads made of extremely fine glass. You will only need to string beads onto the wire to finish this project. That's not hard at all. Simply proceed in accordance with these few directions.

Step 1

Supplies You'll Need

1. Cat Beads

2. Seed Beads

3. Tiger Wire

4. Sterling Silver Jump Rings With Their Ends Closed

5. A lobster claw clasp made of brass

6. Wire Cutter

7. Pliers

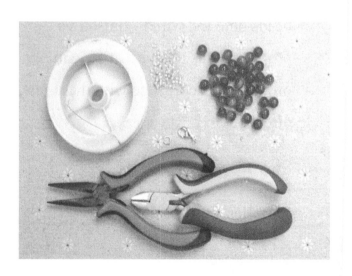

Step 2

Thread Wire for Beading

1. Take a piece of tiger wire that is 100 centimeters long and fold it in half.

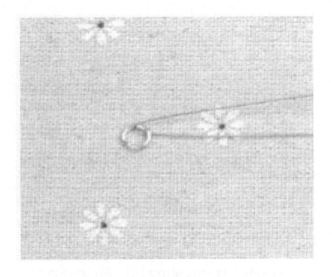

2. Put a jump ring to the middle of the wire, then thread 5 seed beads and one cat eye blue bead one at a time

onto the folded wire in the order that they were listed.

3. If you follow this process and repeat it four times, you will end up with the result shown in the image below.

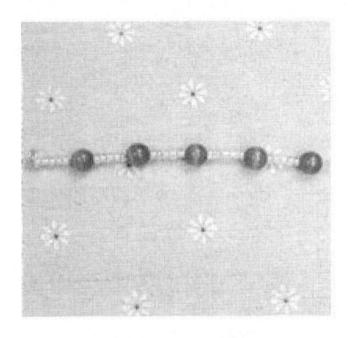

Step 3

Construct the Flower with the Blue Beads

1. Slide 5 seed beads onto both wires, then cross the wire ends through a cat eye blue bead.

2. Add 2 cat eye blue beads to the lower wire and one cat eye bead to the upper wire,

Then cross the wire ends through another cat eye blue bead as shown in the picture below.

Pull the wire to tighten a little

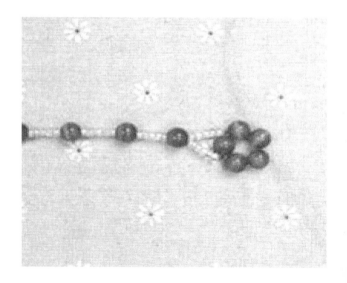

3. Repeat steps 1-2 to complete another 6 blue beaded flowers in the same manner.

Step 4

Make closure by adding Clasp

1. Slip 5 seed beads onto each wire, and then connect the wires together using a cat eye bead;

2. Add another set of 5 seed beads and a cat eye bead to the wire that has been overlapped. Continue to add 5 seed beads and one cat eye bead for a total of 3 times;

3. Secure the brass lobster claw clasp to the wire and trim away any excess wire.

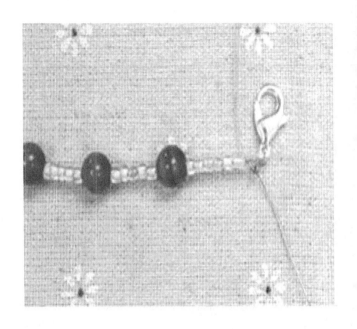

Step 5

Your simple royal beaded necklace is
completed. So lovely to make, wear
and perfect to give as a gift.

CHAPTER TEN

CREATING A ROUND PEARL NECKLACE PENDANT

Here I'm going to show you how to make a necklace that is both lovely, and simple. It's not hard to understand. You will learn how to build a necklace in the shape of a circle using three distinct kinds of beads. They are asymmetrical in appearance and hue, yet when strung together, they create a pleasing pattern. Let's get started immediately!

Step 1

Supplies You'll Need

1. Blue Glass Beads Measuring 8 mm by 6 mm

2. Transparent Seed Beads measuring 4mm

3. 0.8mm Silver Aluminum wire

4. White Pearl Bead measuring 14mm

5. Leather Cord findings

6. Pliers

Step 2

Make the necklace's inner layer.

1. Thread a white pearl bead measuring 14mm onto the aluminum wire.

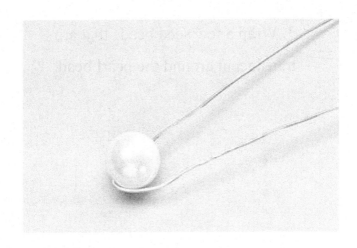

2. Wrap the wire around the base of the pearl bead to create a coil.

3. Wrap a few seed beads that are translucent around the pearl bead.

4. Tie a knot and secure the beads in place.

Step 3

Complete the Necklace's Outer Side.

1. Thread some blue glass beads around the transparent seed beads.

2. Wind the wire around itself and form a loop and cut off the extra wire with the wire cutter.

3. Thread the leather cord findings through the loop created.

Step 4

The necklace has been finished and it will appear like the image shown below.

Note

This pendant pattern may be used to create a pair of matching earrings by simply lowering the amount of beads used in the pendant pattern and

attaching an earring hook to the top
loop.

Conclusion

Bead jewelry designs that are listed in
this book do not need the use of more
complex beading or wire wrapping
techniques. You are able to perform
all of the projects involving beaded
jewelry, regardless of whether you are
an experienced professional or a total
newbie in the art of jewelry making.
Simply proceed in accordance with
the directions that are laid out step by
step in the book. Have the best of
luck!

Made in the USA
Las Vegas, NV
12 January 2024

84280478R00056